OCEAN

Sean Callery

Consultant: David Burnie

KINGFISHER
NEW YORK

KINGFISHER
LONDON & NEW YORK

Copyright © Kingfisher 2011
Published in the United States by Kingfisher,
175 Fifth Ave., New York, NY 10010
Kingfisher is an imprint of Macmillan Children's Books, London.
All rights reserved.

Distributed in the U.S. and Canada by Macmillan,
175 Fifth Ave., New York, NY 10010

Library of Congress Cataloging-in-Publication data has been applied for.

ISBN 978-0-7534-6577-6

Kingfisher books are available for special promotions and premiums.
For details contact: Special Markets Department, Macmillan,
175 Fifth Ave., New York, NY 10010.

For more information, please visit www.kingfisherbooks.com

Printed in China
3 5 7 9 8 6 4 2
2TR/0312/WKT/UNTD/140MA

The publisher would like to thank the following for permission to reproduce their material. Every care has been taken to trace copyright holders. However, if there have been unintentional omissions or failure to trace copyright holders, we apologize and will, if informed, endeavor to make corrections in any future edition.
top = t; bottom = b; center = c; left = l; right = r

All artwork Stuart Jackson-Carter (Peter Kavanagh Art Agency)

Cover c Shutterstock/idreamphoto; cover b Shutterstock/Igor Kovalchuk; cover tl Photolibrary/Peter Arnold Images; cover tcl Naturepl/Wild Wonders of Europe; cover tcr Photolibrary/Animals Animals; cover tr Getty/NGS; back cover Shutterstock/Rich Carey. Page 1 Shutterstock/Calek; 2 Alamy/Premier; 4tr Shutterstock/cbpix; 4bl Naturepl/Andy Rouse; 5tl Shutterstock/Sandy Maya Matzen; 5br Seapics/James D. Watt; 6bl Bluegreenpictures/David Fleetham; 6tr Frank Lane Picture Agency (FLPA)/David Bavendam/Minden; 6br Photolibrary/OSF; 7tl Photolibrary/Waterframe; 7bl Photolibrary/Bios; 7cr Shutterstock/Rui Manuel Teles Gomes; 7tr Shutterstock/frantisekhojdysz; 7ctr FLPA/Chris Newbert/Minden; 7cr FLPA/Hans Leijnse/Minden; 7cbr Photolibrary/Robert Harding; 7cb Shutterstock/Studio 37; 7br Shutterstock/oilas32; 8bl Shutterstock/Mark Doherty; 8blc Getty/Stone; 9tl Naturepl/Georgette Douwa; 9bl Alamy/Danita Delimont; 9tr Shutterstock/Joanna Zopoth-Lipiejko; 9ctr Photolibrary/Tsuneo Nakamura; 9cbr Photolibrary/OSF; 9br Shutterstock/Wallenrock; 9bc Shutterstock/Joze Maucec; 10bl iStockphoto/Boris Tarasov; 11tr Shutterstock/Milena Katzer; 11ctr Corbis/Norbert Wu; 11cr Shutterstock/Olga Khoroshunova; 11bc Shutterstock/Tatiana Belova; 11br Shutterstock/Mark William Penny; 12c Photolibrary/Waterframe; 12bl Image Quest Marine/Masa Ushiod; 13tl Photolibrary/Waterframe 13bl Photolibrary/Waterframe; 13tr Shutterstock/Vlad61; 13ctr Photolibrary/Peter Arnold Images; 13cr Photolibrary/Peter Arnold Images; 13cbr Shutterstock/Undersea Discoveries; 13bc Shutterstock/Geoffrey Lawrence; 13br Shutterstock/A Cotton Photo; 13br Shutterstock/1971yes; 14bl FLPA/Silvestris Fotoservice; 15tl Ardea/Waterframe; 15ctr Getty/NGS; 15cr Getty/NGS; 15cbr Naturepl/David Shale; 15cbr Shutterstock/omers; 15bc Shutterstock/Pavol Kmeto; 16bl Shutterstock/Studio 37; 16blc Seapics; 16br FLPA/D. P. Wilson; 17br FLPA/D. P. Wilson; 17tr Shutterstock/Vlad61; 17cr Naturepl/David Shale; 17cbr Naturepl/David Shale; 17br Shutterstock/michaeljung; 18bl Alamy/Picture Press; 18tr FLPA/Michael Durham/Minden; 18br Alamy/Danita Delimont; 19tl Alamy/Mark Conlin; 19bl Alamy/Lucidio Studio Inc.; 19tr Shutterstock/Chee-Onn Leong; 19ctr Photolibrary/Alaskastock; 19cr Alamy/Mark Conlin; 19cbr Photolibrary/Alaskastock; 19br Shutterstock/bierchen; 20bl Alamy/Steve Bloom; 20tr Alamy/All Canada Photos; 20br Alamy/Christopher Zimmer; 21tl Alamy/Mira; 21bl FLPA/Suzi Eszterhas/Minden; 21tr Shutterstock/Studio 37; 21ctr Shutterstock/Eric Isselee; 21cr Shutterstock/ODM Studio; 21cbr Shutterstock/Robin Phinizy; 21br Shutterstock/Paul Clarke; 21br Shutterstock/Studio 37; 22bl Getty/NGS; 23tr Shutterstock; 23ctr Naturepl/Jurgen Freund; 23cr Getty/Roger Horrocks; 23cbr Naturepl/Jurgen Freund; 23br Shutterstock/D. J. Mattaar; 24bl Seapics/Amar and Isabelle Guillen; 24tr Photolibrary/Peter Arnold Images; 24br Naturepl/Wild Wonders of Europe; 25tl Shutterstock/idreamphoto; 25bl Photolibrary/Animals Animals; 25ctr Photolibrary/Animals Animals; 25cr Naturepl/Ingo Arndt; 25cbr Photoshot/Franco Banfi/NHPA; 25bc Shutterstock/Ocean Image Photography; 25br Shutterstock/Stubblefield Photography; 26bl Photolibrary/Alaskastock; 26tr Seapics/David B. Fleetham; 26br Seapics/Lori Mazzuca; 27tl Photolibrary/All Canada Photos; 27bl Photolibrary/Animals Animals; 27tr Shutterstock/Stephan Kerkhofs; 27ctr Naturepl/Michael S. Nolan; 27cr Naturepl/Doug Perrine; 27cbr Photolibrary/Alaskastock; 27br Photolibrary/Alaskastock; 27br Shutterstock/Nikita Tiunov; 27bc Shutterstock/frantisekhojdsz

Contents

Introduction

The oceans of the world are home to millions of amazing animals—from the largest on Earth to some of the tiniest, too small for us to see with the naked eye.

All these living things need to eat to stay alive. Some make their own food using the Sun's energy, some eat plants, and many try to eat one another. The list of who eats who is called a food chain.

The first animal in a food chain is called a primary consumer because it eats other living things. This clown fish, for example, eats algae and other sea animals.

NORTH AMERICA

Atlantic Ocean

equator

SOUTH AMERICA

South Pacific Ocean

Most food chains start with things that make their own food using the Sun's energy. They are known as producers and include seaweed (left) and algae called phytoplankton, which drift in the oceans.

Next in a food chain is what is known as a secondary consumer. It might be a carnivore or an omnivore. Puffins are secondary consumers that eat fish and small sea animals.

This book takes you through three food chains from oceans in different parts of the world. You will find out about the life cycles of 11 animals: how they are born, grow, reproduce, and die.

Arctic Ocean

EUROPE

ASIA

AFRICA

North Pacific Ocean

Indian Ocean

AUSTRALIA

Southern Ocean

At the top of a food chain is an animal like this swordfish, which has no predators because it is so fast and fierce.

ANTARCTICA

Coral

Coral reefs grow mostly in warm waters such as the tropical oceans around the equator. They are built up by tiny animals called polyps. The hard, chalky cups in which the polyps grow are left behind when they die and form the coral rock.

1 Coral polyps reproduce in two ways. The first way is by producing eggs. The females release the eggs into the water, and the males fertilize them.

2 Tiny larvae hatch from the eggs and drift in the water. Soon they land on hard surfaces such as rocks and attach themselves there.

4 Coral polyps also reproduce by splitting in half. They divide again and again until there is an entire colony of polyps.

3 The larvae grow into polyps. Their bodies are like small bags with tentacles at one end for catching prey. The polyps grow bigger until they can produce eggs themselves.

Did you know?

Corals can be all sorts of shapes. Some look like mushrooms; others look like cones or even cabbages!

Many sea animals sneak into gaps in the coral to hide from predators—or wait there to pounce on prey.

Coral reefs protect some coasts. They slow down the ocean so that big waves hit the land less hard and do less damage.

Coral reefs can be hundreds or even thousands of years old, but coral polyps are eaten in huge numbers by one animal . . .

Crown-of-thorns starfish

Crown-of-thorns starfish eat coral. They crawl across the reef sucking up the coral polyps and leaving dead coral rock behind them.

1 The female starfish release millions of eggs, and the males fertilize them. This is called spawning.

2 The eggs develop into larvae, which drift in the water and feed on tiny plantlike algae.

4 The starfish grow more arms. After six months they are as big as your fingernail. Full-grown adults can be 14 inches (35cm) across.

3 The larvae settle on rocks, the seabed, shipwrecks, or coral reefs. In two days, they change into small starfish with arms. Now they can move around.

Did you know?

 A crown-of-thorns starfish is covered in prickly spines that can cut attackers and leave them with terrible wounds.

 A crown-of-thorns starfish can have up to 23 arms. It can grow a new arm if one is bitten off or damaged.

 A starfish eats by pushing its stomach out through its mouth. The folds of the stomach wrap around the prey and digest it.

Crown-of-thorns starfish can live for eight years, but there is one predator that is not hurt by their spines . . .

Puffer fish

Puffer fish are slow swimmers, so they scare away predators by blowing themselves up to look bigger than they are. If that fails, the poison in their bodies makes them a very nasty mouthful to eat.

1 When they mate, the male fish pushes the female up to the water's surface, where she lays her eggs. He fertilizes them as they float in the water.

2 The eggs hatch into larvae. Each larva has a bag of food, called a yolk sac, attached to its body. The food keeps it alive until it is able to catch prey.

4 Adult puffer fish can be 20 inches (50cm) long. They live in warm waters and can survive for more than five years, eating starfish, crabs, fish, and plants.

3 Over the next ten days, the larvae grow into young fish, called fry. They can now feed themselves. As they grow, they develop white spots and stripes on their skin.

When a puffer fish is scared, it fills its stretchy stomach with water until it is big and round like a balloon.

Puffer fish have hidden spines that stick up when the fish inflates. These make it difficult to swallow.

A puffer fish has a strong beak made of four teeth joined together.

A puffer fish's poison can kill, but some predators will eat it and take that risk . . .

Tiger shark

Tiger sharks are deadly hunters. They usually swim slowly and can get close to prey undetected. Then they put on a burst of speed and grab the prey before it can escape.

1 The female tiger shark mates with a male every three years. Up to 80 eggs develop into embryos in her womb, each with a yolk sac attached to its body.

2 After 16 months, the shark gives birth to a litter of babies, called pups. They swim away and must take care of themselves right from the start.

4 It takes many years for sharks to reach adulthood. They can be 15 years old before they are able to mate.

3 Young tiger sharks have dark stripes on their bodies, which is how the fish gets its name. These markings fade as the sharks grow.

Did you know?

When a shark attacks, its eyelids cover its eyes to protect them from being damaged.

Some sharks have to swim all the time or they will drown. Swimming forces water through their gills so they can breathe.

A shark's jaws are lined with rows of sharp, triangular teeth. If one tooth breaks, another is ready to take its place.

Tiger sharks are at the top of many food chains. No one knows for certain, but they may live for up to 40 years.

Pink shrimp

Pink shrimp are small, shelled sea animals. They live in the cold parts of the Pacific and Atlantic oceans, eating tiny animals and plants. They in turn are food for many other animals in the ocean.

1 The female shrimp carries thousands of eggs on her back legs until they hatch into larvae. Then she releases them.

2 The see-through larvae float freely in the water and start to eat algae.

Did you know?

Shrimp swim by flicking their tails forward underneath their bodies. This pushes them backward through the water.

4 The juvenile shrimp are all males at this stage, but within a year they will change into females. When the ocean temperature is right, they will lay their eggs and start the life cycle again.

They have two pairs of antennae, which they use to feel around for food or to detect danger.

3 After about four days, the larvae change shape to become more like adult shrimp, although they are still see-through.

Pink shrimp have ten pairs of legs. The front five pairs are for walking and feeding; the others are for swimming.

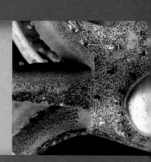

Pink shrimp can live for four years, but only a few survive this long. Many other animals like to munch on them . . .

Black-eyed squid

Black-eyed squids are jet-propelled sea animals. Their bodies are like bags with eight arms and two longer tentacles, which they use to reach out and grab their prey. They live mostly deep down in the ocean.

1 Most squids lay their eggs on the seabed, but the female black-eyed squid carries all 2,000–3,000 of them around with her in a sac as big as her body.

2 The eggs are held together in a special jelly. The female squid uses her arms to clean them and to keep the water moving around them.

4 As the babies leave to feed and grow into adults, the female squid is so tired and hungry that she dies.

3 It takes six to nine months for the eggs to hatch. During this time, the female squid stays with them and does not eat.

Did you know?

Squids confuse attackers by shooting a cloud of dark ink into their eyes. This gives the squids a chance to escape.

A squid's eyes face in opposite directions. This gives it good all-around vision.

A squid's arms and tentacles are covered with suckers, which it uses to grab prey and pull it into its mouth.

Black-eyed squids can live for two years, but many are snapped up by other animals before then . . .

Coho salmon

Coho salmon, also called silver salmon, spend part of their lives in the ocean. Then they go on an amazing journey, swimming upriver to return to the place where they were born.

1 The female digs a nest in the gravel bed of a stream. She lays thousands of eggs, which are fertilized by males, and then she covers them up. She does this a few times. The eggs hatch after several months.

2 The hatchlings stay in the nest for up to two weeks. They hardly move, and they live on their yolk sacs—bags of food attached to their bodies.

18

4 Adult coho salmon stay in the ocean for between one and three years. Then they swim back to where they were born. Not even waterfalls will stop them. Once there, they mate, lay their eggs, and die.

3 The hatchlings grow into young fish and start to eat tiny insects and plants. They will live in fresh water for about a year before they swim downriver to the salty ocean.

Did you know?

A salmon is shaped like a rocket to move smoothly through the water. Its eight fins help it stay balanced.

Some experts believe that salmon use their sense of smell to find their way back to the river where they were born.

Coho salmon develop bright red sides when they swim into fresh water.

Very few salmon complete their incredible journey. There are many predators in the water—and also in the air . . .

Bald eagle

Bald eagles are huge birds of prey with sharp talons and hooked beaks. They glide over oceans and rivers, swooping down to grab fish.

1 Bald eagles mate for life. They build nests high up in tall trees, on cliffs near the coast, or beside rivers and expand them each year.

2 Females lay up to three eggs, and the parents take turns guarding the nest. They sit on the eggs to keep them warm for about 35 days.

20

4 The young eagles first start to fly when they are about 12 weeks old, but they live in the nest for another eight weeks while they learn how to hunt.

3 Then the chicks hatch. They are too weak to stand up until they are four to five weeks old. They are always hungry and open their big beaks every time a parent returns to the nest.

Did you know?

Eagles see five times better than humans. They are able to spot a fish in shallow water 1 mile (1.6km) away.

Eagles lift a fish out of the water using their strong, sharp talons. They hold it with one foot and tear it apart with their beak.

If a bald eagle catches a fish that it cannot lift, it paddles to the shore using its wings.

Bald eagles are so big and fierce that they are at the top of many food chains. They live for about 30 years.

Box jellyfish

Box jellyfish look like harmless blobs, but their tentacles carry a powerful sting for catching prey. They swim through tropical waters eating crustaceans and fish.

1 The females release their eggs into shallow water near the coast. The males fertilize the eggs.

2 Tiny larvae hatch and sink down until they land on a surface such as a rock or the seabed. There, they develop into polyps with tentacles.

4 The polyps grow into tiny jellyfish, called medusas. They leave the seabed and float away to feed until they become adults and are ready to breed.

3 The polyps trap prey in their tentacles. Over many months, the polyps grow buds, and more new polyps grow out of the buds. Soon there is a small colony of polyps.

Did you know?

Box jellyfish have four sets of tentacles. Each one of these tentacles has 500,000 poisonous stinging cells.

Unlike other jellyfish, box jellyfish swim well and steer toward the light. Other jellyfish simply drift.

A jellyfish has one opening underneath its umbrella-like bell. Food comes in and waste goes out through it.

Box jellyfish live for about a year. They are attacked by larger animals that are not harmed by their poisonous stings . . .

Sea turtle

Loggerhead turtles are champion divers: they can stay underwater for up to four hours. They paddle around the oceans, feeding on plants and other animals, including jellyfish.

1 At night, the female comes to the flat, sandy beach where she was born. She lays about 100 eggs and covers them up. She does this about four times in each mating season.

2 The babies grow inside the eggs for about 80 days. Then they break out of the shells using a special sharp egg tooth that they lose afterward.

Did you know?

Turtles have no teeth. Instead, they have beaklike mouths and spines in their throats to stop their prey from escaping.

Turtles pull themselves through the water with their long front flippers and use the back ones to steer.

A turtle's red-brown shell is called a carapace. Sometimes small animals, such as barnacles, live on it.

4 When they are more than 17 years old, the adult females return to the same beach to lay their eggs. They will do this every two to three years. The males never come ashore again.

3 The hatchlings look for the bright light of the moon shining on the ocean and crawl across the sand toward it. Then they swim out into the ocean.

Loggerhead turtles can live for 50 years. They are so big that only animals with large mouths can attack them . . .

Killer whale

Killer whales, or orcas, are sometimes called the "wolves of the sea" because they hunt in packs. They eat anything they can catch, including sea turtles.

1 Killer whales mate every five years, and the females have one baby at a time. The baby grows inside its mother's womb for 15–18 months.

2 A baby killer whale, or calf, is born with black and yellow skin. It gradually sheds this skin, and the yellow areas change to white.

4 Killer whales live in groups called pods. Calves remain with their pod for years; female calves stay forever. A pod might have a grandmother, her daughter, and her daughter's calves in it.

3 Like all mammal babies, a killer whale calf needs its mother's milk. It feeds several times an hour, 24 hours a day, for a year.

Did you know?

The dorsal fin helps the killer whale turn and stay upright. A male's dorsal fin can be 6.5 feet (2m) high.

Killer whales have between 40 and 56 teeth. Each tooth is 3 inches (7.5cm) long and curved to help it grip prey.

Killer whales breathe air through a blowhole in the top of their head. When they dive, a flap stops water from getting in.

Killer whales live for about 50 years. No other animal attacks them, so they are at the top of many food chains.

An Atlantic food web

This book follows three ocean food chains. Most animals eat more than one food, however, so they are part of several food chains. There are many food chains in an ocean, and they link like a map to make a food web.

sailfish

seagull

killer whale

sea turtle

shark

crab

jellyfish

clam

plankton

Sun

mackerel

sea horse

This is a food web from
the Atlantic Ocean.

Glossary

ALGAE
Plantlike living things that make their food using the Sun's energy.

ANTENNAE
A pair of feelers on a shrimp's head.

CARNIVORE
An animal that eats other animals.

CONSUMER
A living thing that survives by eating other living things.

CRUSTACEAN
A group of animals that includes shrimp and crabs. They have three main body parts and an external skeleton.

DIGEST
When the body breaks down food to get the nutrients that will keep it alive.

EMBRYO
An early form of a baby animal growing inside its mother.

FERTILIZE
When sperm from a male animal meets the egg of a female to make a new life.

FIN
The part of a fish's body that helps it stay balanced and steer through the water.

FRESH WATER
Water that is not salty like seawater.

GILLS
The organs used to breathe underwater.

HATCHLING
An animal just born from a hard-shelled egg.

INFLATE
To fill with air or water.

JUVENILE
Another word for young.

LARVA
A young animal that will change its body shape to become an adult. Groups are called larvae.

MATE
When a male and female animal reproduce. For some animals, there is a particular time each year when they mate, and this is called the "mating season."

OMNIVORE
An animal that eats plants and other animals.

PLANKTON
Tiny living things that drift in seas and oceans. If they are plants, they are called phytoplankton. If they are animals, they are called zooplankton.

POD
A group of whales.

POISON
A substance that harms living things.

POLYP
An animal with a soft body and a mouth surrounded by tentacles.

PREDATOR
An animal that kills and eats other animals.

PREY
An animal that is hunted by a predator.

PRODUCER
A living thing that makes its own food from the energy of the Sun.

SAC
A bag of food attached to a baby animal, or a bag of eggs (see the black-eyed squid).

SPAWNING
When sea animals release their eggs to be fertilized.

SUCKER
A cup-shaped part of an animal's arm, used for gripping things.

TALON
A bird's claw.

TENTACLE
A long, thin arm usually used for gripping and feeding.

TROPICAL
Describes oceans around the equator where the water is warmer because it gets the most sunshine.

WOMB
The part of a female animal where babies grow.

YOLK
The nutrients inside an egg that feed a new baby animal.

These websites have information about oceans or their animals—or both!

- animaldiversity.ummz.umich.edu/site/index.html
- bbc.co.uk/nature/blueplanet
- earthskids.com/ek_science-marine.htm
- enchantedlearning.com/subjects/ocean
- iiseagrant.org/NabInvader
- ocean.nationalgeographic.com/ocean
- pbskids.org/wildkratts/habitats/ocean
- thekidswindow.co.uk/News/Oceans_Quiz.htm

Index

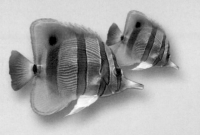